The Story of
CIVIL WAR HERO
ROBERT SMALLS

by **Janet Halfmann**
illustrated by **Duane Smith**

Lee & Low Books Inc.
New York

In memory of the thousands of African Americans
who helped win the Civil War—J.H.

To the men and women in the armed forces who are
serving abroad in the Middle East, for your bravery.
To my family and friends for support. I thank the Lord
for blessing the works of my hands.—D.S.

Author's Acknowledgments: I wish to especially thank Kitt Alexander, founder of the Robert Smalls Legacy Foundation, for help with research sources and for reading the manuscript. I also wish to thank Richard W. Hatcher III, Historian, Fort Sumter National Monument, for answering questions. Thanks also to the Amistad Research Center, Beaufort County Library, Robert Smalls Middle School, Wilberforce University Archives and Special Collections, The New York Public Library, University of Wisconsin-Milwaukee Libraries, and the Milwaukee County Federated Library System, for providing reference materials. A special thanks to my editor Momo Sanya for helping me bring Robert Smalls's story to life—J.H.

Text copyright © 2008, 2020 by Janet Halfmann
Illustrations copyright © 2008 by Duane Smith
For photo credits, see page 80.

LEE & LOW BOOKS Inc., 95 Madison Avenue, New York, NY 10016
leeandlow.com
Edited by Momo Sanya and Cheryl Klein
Book design by Charice Silverman and NeuStudio
Book production by The Kids at Our House
The text is set in Avenir and Vollkorn.
The illustrations are rendered in oil on paper.

10 9 8 7 6 5 4 3 2 1
First Edition

MIX
Paper from
responsible sources
FSC
www.fsc.org   FSC® C020691

Cataloging-in-Publication Data is on file with the Library of Congress.

TABLE OF CONTENTS

CHAPTER ONE
DREAMS OF FREEDOM

Robert Smalls's dreams of freedom began in his hometown of Beaufort, South Carolina, the largest town on a cluster of plantation islands down the coast from Charleston. He was born there in 1839 in the slave quarters on the McKee family's property.

Robert's mother was a house servant, and when he was about six years old, Robert also began working in the McKee household. He brushed Master McKee's horse, carried his hunting bow, and baited his fishing hook. Good-spirited and talkative, Robert was the master's favorite.

As a favored house servant, Robert had an easier life than most enslaved people. Even so, from the time he was a young boy, he witnessed the evils of slavery. At neighboring plantations he saw enslaved people whipped until they were bloody, punished for the simplest things, like getting to the fields a few moments late, missing a patch of weeds, or not working fast enough. In town Robert watched boys and girls his own age sold like animals on the **auction** block.

Although the McKees were kind to him, Robert grew to hate slavery. More and more he wished to be free.

Slavery

Slavery has existed in various forms around the world throughout history. Many people became enslaved by being captured in wars between nations or tribes. Others were enslaved until they could pay off a debt.

When the English settled in America in the early 1600s, tobacco soon became a major source of income, which meant lots of workers were needed in the fields. At first, **planters** used **indentured servants**— mostly white, but also black. Poor and often young, the indentured servants worked for four to seven years in exchange for travel to America. But once they served their time, they were free.

Planters gradually switched to slave labor, partly because indentured workers became less plentiful, but mostly because it was easier and more profitable to use workers who would be forced to labor their whole lives for no pay. White landowners first tried to enslave Native Americans, but they died of European diseases or ran away. So increasingly planters relied on enslaved black people kidnapped and shipped from West Africa under cruel, crowded conditions.

As the number of enslaved black workers in the colonies grew, their treatment became harsher and

SECTIONS OF A SLAVE SHIP.

This 1830 image of the Brazilian ship *Veloz* shows how the kidnapped and enslaved people were packed tightly into an area above the hold. This small ship carried as many as 550 enslaved people from Africa to Brazil.

harsher, and white people often chose to see them as subhuman in order to **justify** the cruelty. Starting in 1662 in Virginia, the colonies passed laws that made slavery in America especially crushing. These laws declared that all children born to enslaved mothers were enslaved for life, and that the enslaved were property, like a chair or hammer—a system called **chattel slavery**. This system meant white planters could treat enslaved people any way they wanted without fear of punishment, and owners could increase their slave holdings and wealth from generation to generation through new births, sales, and inheritance.

At one time, slavery was legal in all the American colonies. Though numbers in the northern colonies were relatively low, the North played a major role in the slave trade because it controlled the shipping industry. The number of enslaved in the southern colonies kept growing because more and more workers were needed for the area's **agricultural economy**. After the American Revolution, many northern states banned slavery, while white southerners increasingly saw slavery as necessary to their way of life, giving them wealth and **prestige**.

Most of the enslaved in the South worked on plantations, which varied widely in size. The largest plantations were like small villages, with the enslaved doing any task needed, from weaving to blacksmithing. Daily life for field and house workers differed greatly. **Field hands** worked from sunup to sundown planting and harvesting crops such as cotton, rice, and tobacco. If they didn't work fast enough, they would be whipped. Their clothes often were ragged and food was scarce and of poor quality. Enslaved people who worked in the house, like Robert Smalls's mother, generally had better clothes and more to eat. They cooked, cleaned, and took care of the master's children. Meanwhile, enslaved people who lived in cities might be hired out by their owners to work as carpenters, shipbuilders, bakers, or in other trades.

Besides providing free labor, enslaved people themselves were worth a lot of money to their owners. Prime field hands sold for $400 to $600 in 1800, $1300 to $1500 in 1850, and up to $3000 by 1860. Due to the inherited nature of chattel slavery, the number of enslaved blacks kept growing, from just over one million in 1805 to about four million in 1860 on the eve of the Civil War. This allowed white slave owners to build considerable wealth at the expense of the lives of the enslaved.

This drawing from the 1860 *Children's Anti-Slavery Book* illustrates the breakup of an enslaved family due to white greed.

Southerners often argued that enslaved people were content, and that slavery was good for all involved. The enslaved proved those views false again and again. In the two hundred years before the Civil War, there were more than 250 successful or attempted slave uprisings. The size of the rebellions varied from ten people to thousands. Three of the largest were led by Gabriel Prosser in 1800 and Nat Turner in 1831, both in Virginia, and Denmark Vesey in South Carolina in 1822.

Many other enslaved people escaped singly or with a few others. Escapees often received help from the Underground Railroad, a network of blacks and whites that provided shelter, food, and other aid to those on the run. By the time the Civil War started in 1861, more than sixty thousand enslaved had escaped to freedom in the North.

CHAPTER TWO
ON THE WATERFRONT

In 1851, when Robert was twelve, the McKees sent him to live and work in Charleston. All day and into the night he waited tables and made deliveries to rooms at the elegant Planter's Hotel. Robert earned five dollars a month but had to give the money to his master.

Anytime Robert wasn't working he headed to the waterfront. He watched the ships of all shapes and sizes, fascinated by how they could sail anywhere in the world.

Robert liked talking to the workers on the ships. In hushed voices, they told him stories about "Up North," where all black people were free to learn to read and write. Free to keep the money they earned. Free to make their own decisions. Robert's eyes lit up with hope. Someday he would have those freedoms too.

Eager to spend more time at the waterfront, Robert got permission from Master McKee to work at the docks loading and unloading **cargo** from ships. Robert worked hard. He was smart and dependable, and by age fifteen he was **foreman** of a crew, directing men twice his age.

Eventually Robert grew to dislike the routine of the job, so he moved to the shipyard and began making and **rigging** sails. Robert enjoyed testing the sails on boats in the water, and he learned to **navigate** narrow **channels**, gliding carefully past hidden rocks. His boss boasted that Robert had the makings of a wheelman, the title given to black boat pilots in the South.

Sailing Ships in the 1800s

On a typical day in Charleston Harbor, South Carolina, in the early 1800s, more than a hundred sailing ships lined the docks.

There were many types of ships, but they all had *hulls*, or bodies, made of strong wood, and usually one to three tall masts to hold up their sails. It might take 2,000 or more trees to build a large ship. The force of the wind on the sails moved the ship along.

The sails on a sailing ship can be arranged in two basic ways. In a *square rig*, rectangular sails sit squarely across the masts. They run most efficiently when being pushed from behind by the wind. In a *fore-and-aft* or *schooner rig*, triangular sails lie along the length of the ship, allowing them to catch winds coming from many directions. Some ships have both kinds of rig.

Square-rigged ships were slow and designed for heavy cargo. In the 1800s, they carried rice and cotton from Charleston to European markets. Schooners could move more quickly and sail in both deep oceans

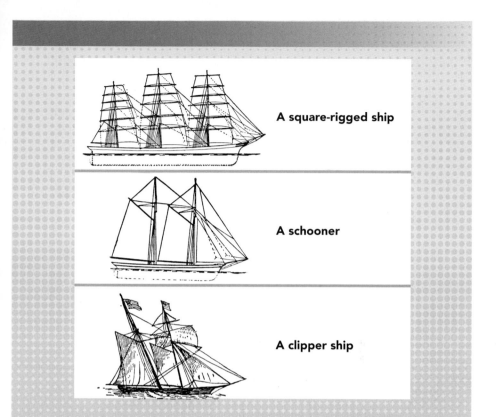

A square-rigged ship

A schooner

A clipper ship

and shallow coastal and inland waters. Robert Smalls's summer work on a coastal schooner helped to develop his early piloting skills.

Schooners were fast, but by the 1840s, traders wanted still more speed. Everyone wanted to be first to deliver each new season's crop of tea from China to customers. Thus, the speedy, elegant *clipper ships* were born. Clippers featured tall, angled masts, a square rig, and a very long, slim hull. This design allowed clippers to carry so many sails that they could keep moving even in calm weather. The crew of a clipper might number up to a hundred. It would include the captain and other officers, a cook, and sailors to maintain and operate the ship. Larger ships might have a sail maker, a carpenter, and crews from around the world.

In addition to sailing ships, steamboats—powered by steam engines and paddle wheels—churned in Charleston Harbor and other ports. These smaller vessels, built for river travel, became popular soon after Robert Fulton built the first **commercially** successful steamboat in 1807. Before long, steam engines were added to sailing ships to prevent them from having to rely on the wind. The first Atlantic crossing by a sailing ship with a steam engine and paddle wheels was the *Savannah* in 1819. Nineteen years later, in 1838, a ship called the *Sirius* became the first to cross the Atlantic completely by steam.

Soon propellers replaced paddle wheels on steamships. Propellers were more efficient, less bulky, and not as likely to be damaged as the enormous paddle

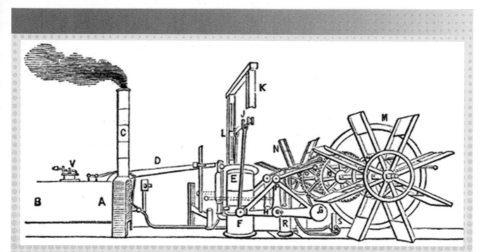

A diagram of the boiler for Robert Fulton's 1807 steamship. The engineer fed coal into the firebox (A), which created heat that fed through the pipe (D) to heat water in the boiler (E). The water turned to steam, and the force of the steam powered the gears (G) and finally the paddle wheels (M, N).

wheels. Paddle wheels, however, worked better than propellers in shallow water, so they continued to be used on lake and river steamboats.

Eventually iron began to replace wood for building ships. The first steamship to be built entirely of iron was the *Great Britain* in 1843. Still later, steel would replace iron. By the 1860s, the speedier, more efficient steamships were on their way to taking over the seas. The centuries-long "Age of Sail" was nearing its end.

CHAPTER THREE
A SHELTER
IN THE STORM

When Robert was seventeen he met Hannah Jones, a Charleston hotel maid with sparkling eyes and an intelligence to match his own. She was owned by Samuel Kingman. In order to marry and live together, the couple worked out agreements with their masters. Robert and Hannah would find their own jobs. Every month Robert would give McKee fifteen dollars, and Hannah would give Kingman seven dollars. Any other money the couple earned would be their own.

Robert and Hannah married on December 24, 1856, and in February 1858, their first child, Elizabeth, was born. As Robert held the tiny bundle, he was saddened by the realization that Elizabeth did not belong to them. She was the property of Hannah's master. So Robert made a deal to buy his wife's and daughter's freedom for eight hundred dollars. Although Robert was still enslaved, the arrangement would allow Hannah and Elizabeth to go wherever he went.

Robert and Hannah didn't know how they would save that much money, but they were going to try. In the evenings, by candlelight, Hannah sewed **garments** for the wealthy women of Charleston while Robert studied maps and charts of the harbor, rivers, creeks, and channels. He noted the location of every **reef**, sandbar, and current. Soon he was expertly navigating the waterways, delivering boats to plantations all along the coast. During summers, Robert worked as a sailor on a coastal schooner. His dedication and skill earned him a reputation as one of the best boat handlers in Charleston.

After three years the couple saved seven hundred dollars. Robert and Hannah were close to their goal, but a storm was brewing in the nation.

By the fall of 1860, Charleston was at the eye of the storm. For a long time, northern and southern states had been arguing about slavery. As the country expanded west, southerners wanted slavery allowed in the new **territories**. Northerners did not. In November 1860 Abraham Lincoln, who opposed the spread of slavery, was elected president. South Carolina responded by breaking away from the United States. Several other southern states followed. Together, they formed the **Confederate States of America**.

The northern states remained the United States of America, or the Union.

The Confederacy quickly took charge of many military forts in the South, but the Union kept control of Fort Sumter in Charleston Harbor. On April 12, 1861, a battle for Fort Sumter ended in the fort's surrender to the Confederacy. A civil war between the North and South had begun.

For enslaved people such as Robert and Hannah war brought uncertainty, but also hope. If the North won, slavery would end.

What Caused the Civil War?

The bitter division that led to the Civil War between the Northern and Southern United States from 1861– 1865 was a long time in the making. Even when they were English colonies, the two areas differed greatly. The South's economy depended mainly on agriculture. The North relied mostly on selling goods at home and around the world.

Slavery became a **divisive** issue early on. In 1787, when the leaders of the newly formed United States drafted the **Constitution**, seven hundred thousand people—18 percent of the new nation's population— were enslaved, most living in the South. Slavery had become so important to the southern economy that many white people believed the South could not survive without it. Founding leaders including George Washington, Thomas Jefferson, and James Madison all were slave owners. But many northern states had already begun to ban slavery, and other founding leaders, like John Adams, were deeply opposed to it.

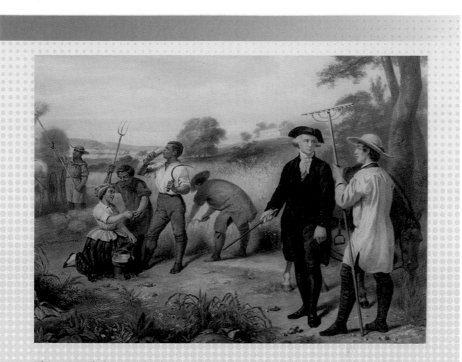

This 1853 lithograph shows George Washington with a few of the 317 people who labored in slavery on his Virginia estate.

Since the founders' main goal was to create a new government, they compromised on the issue of slavery. The final Constitution protected the international slave trade until 1808, required **fugitive** enslaved people to be returned to their masters, and otherwise allowed slavery to continue where it already existed.

As many people immigrated to the United States and the country expanded westward, the issue of slavery steadily became more divisive. The North grew more and more **industrialized.** Immigrants from Ireland and Germany streamed to northern cities, providing plenty of people to work for low wages. The South, where cotton was the main export, required lots of hands working in the fields. Free labor meant larger profits. Southern slaveholders argued falsely that enslaved blacks were content and better off than they would be on their own. Enslaved people constantly proved their owners wrong by resisting in many ways, such as secretly learning to read (even though it was against the law) or running away.

From 1787 to 1819, an uneasy **truce** existed between the North and South on the slavery issue, with eleven states on each side. That changed when Missouri wanted to enter the Union as a slave state. To maintain the balance, the Missouri Compromise of 1820 admitted Maine as a free state. The new law established the border between Pennsylvania and Maryland, also known as the *Mason-Dixon line*, as the boundary north of which no more slave states would be allowed.

As time passed, more and more white northerners

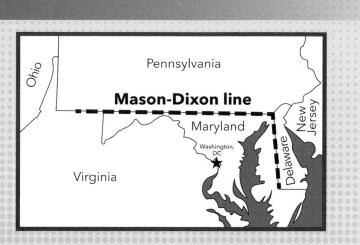

Pennsylvania

Ohio

Mason-Dixon line

Maryland

New Jersey

Washington, DC

Delaware

Virginia

The Mason-Dixon line symbolically divides the northern and southern United States. (West Virginia did not become its own state until 1863.)

came to believe slavery was morally wrong. More and more white southerners disagreed. Each conflict in Congress increased tensions. In the Compromise of 1850, California came into the Union as a free state. To counter that gain for the North, a law called the Fugitive Slave Act was made much stronger. It forced officials in all states to arrest runaways, and **penalized** anyone who helped in their escape. Four years later, the Kansas-Nebraska Act basically did away with the Missouri Compromise. It allowed residents of new US territories to decide via popular vote whether to allow slavery in their state. This enraged northerners,

Free and Slave States and Territories in 1858

Washington Territory
Oregon Territory
Nebraska Territory
Unorganized Territory
Minnesota
Wisconsin
Michigan
New Hampshire
Vermont
Maine
New York
Massachusetts
Rhode Island
Connecticut
Iowa
Pennsylvania
New Jersey
Utah Territory
Illinois
Indiana
Ohio
Delaware
Kansas Territory
Virginia
Maryland
District of Columbia
California
Missouri
Kentucky
North Carolina
New Mexico Territory
Indian Territory
Arkansas
Tennessee
South Carolina
Texas
Georgia
Louisiana
Alabama
Florida
Mississippi

Slave states   Free states   Territories

because slavery might now move above the Mason-Dixon line.

With the country in crisis, Abraham Lincoln, who opposed the spread of slavery, was elected president in November 1860. Even though he said he had no plans to **abolish** slavery, white southerners didn't believe him. Without even waiting for Lincoln's **inauguration**, seven southern states broke away from the United States to form the Confederate States of America. Later, four more states would **secede**.

Lincoln maintained that it was against the law for any state to leave the Union. He vowed to keep the United States together. Words changed to action when the Confederacy ordered American forces to surrender Fort Sumter in Charleston Harbor because it was on southern soil. When the Americans refused, the Confederates moved to take the fort on April 12, 1861, firing the first shots of what would become the Civil War.

CHAPTER FOUR

ROBERT AT THE WHEEL

Commercial shipping traffic in and out of Charleston Harbor had slowed to a trickle. Since there was no work for Robert in the shipyard, he had taken a job as wheelman on the *Planter*, a 147-foot, wood-burning steamer. The boat once hauled cotton but had been converted into an armed Confederate vessel for carrying soldiers, equipment, and supplies.

All that summer on the *Planter* Robert helped build up Confederate defenses in the harbor and along the coast. He laid mines, destroyed a lighthouse, and built new forts. But in his heart Robert wanted the Union to win the war.

Robert's navigational skills and knowledge of the waterways impressed the *Planter*'s officers.

Being the wheelman was a position of trust and honor. Responsible for steering the boat, Robert learned the secret steam whistle signals for passing the harbor's many forts.

In late 1861 freedom suddenly grew closer for Robert and Hannah. The Union navy captured Port Royal, just down the coast from Charleston. A Union fleet set up a **blockade** at the entrance to Charleston Harbor. Looking through the captain's field glasses, Robert could see the northern ships. The Union lines and freedom were within reach—only seven miles away.

This gave Robert renewed hope and determination, as did the birth of his son, Robert Jr. Now more than ever, Robert knew he had to find a way to freedom, for himself and his growing family.

When the opportunity finally came, it started with a joke. One evening the boat's white officers went ashore to spend the night, even though this was against military rules. Jokingly, one of the crew plopped the captain's straw hat on Robert's head. Robert crossed his arms and strutted about just like the short, strongly built captain. Everyone laughed. Given Robert's similar build, the resemblance was amazing.

Suddenly Robert became serious and told the men to keep the joke to themselves. He had an idea.

Robert shared his plan with Hannah. On a night when the officers were ashore, he and the crew would steal the *Planter*. Their families would hide at a nearby **wharf** and be picked up on the way. Wearing the captain's hat and responding with the secret steam whistle signals,

Robert would trick the fort guards into letting the boat pass. He would sail the *Planter* out to the Union fleet—and to freedom.

Hannah asked him what would happen if they were caught. Robert told her they would probably be shot. Hannah was quiet for a moment, and then agreed to go along. She too was willing to risk her life and the lives of their children for a chance at freedom.

Robert explained the plan to his crewmates and made them promise to keep it secret. He also told them that if something went wrong, they would sink the boat rather than be captured. If it didn't go down fast enough, they would all clasp hands and jump overboard. The men agreed. They trusted Robert, and they too yearned for freedom.

The timing was left to Robert. He had to choose the right moment.

The *Planter*

The *Planter,* completed in late 1860, was still brand-new when Robert Smalls became its wheelman. Originally built to carry cotton and passengers, it was considered the speediest boat out of Charleston Harbor, South Carolina.

The boat was built in Charleston of red cedar and live oak. Live oak is a strong tree famous for shipbuilding and common to southern coasts. The body or hull of the boat measured 147 feet long and 30 feet wide, with three decks rising above the water. It could haul up to 1,200 bales of cotton from plantations to the wharves. It also had several cabins for passengers and crew. Copper covered the bottom to protect it from decay and water creatures. The *Planter* could travel in water less than four feet deep. That made it perfect for easy, fast travel along South Carolina's shallow coast and through the area's twisting rivers and creeks.

The *Planter* was a steamboat, or steamer, with furnaces that burned wood, which was plentiful along the

The *Planter* loaded with one thousand bales of cotton, sometime between 1866 and 1876.

area's waterways. The fire heated water in two boilers on the main deck. Boilers are large metal containers filled with water. When the water in the *Planter*'s boilers was heated, it turned to steam, which then powered the boat's two engines. These engines drove two side wooden paddle wheels. Wooden boxes around the paddle wheels kept water from spraying on the boat. The *Planter*'s two engines could spin the paddle wheels in opposite directions, allowing the steamer to turn on a dime! (Steamers with paddle wheels on both sides are called *side-wheelers*; those with a paddle wheel at the rear are called *stern-wheelers*.) The crew on the *Planter*, and all steamers, kept a close eye on the boilers to make sure too much pressure didn't build up inside. Boiler explosions, often deadly, were a huge danger facing steamboats of the time.

When the *Planter* was **leased** to the Confederates, it became General Roswell Ripley's personal dispatch boat for relaying military messages. The steamer also carried supplies, men, and equipment around the harbor and surrounding area. Large guns were added on both decks for protection. Under the Confederates, Robert Smalls was part of a crew of ten, including three white officers: the captain, a first mate, and an engineer. Robert served as wheelman, and six other enslaved black men acted as engineers and deckhands.

The *Planter*'s pilothouse, also called the wheel-house, sat high above the water, right over the boilers. Robert steered the boat from there. Piloting the boat took great skill to avoid dangerous currents and sandbars that might wreck the steamer. Steamboat pilothouses often had ropes to pull that led to signal bells in the engine room and on deck. Each bell gave a different signal. Often a speaking tube allowed the pilot to talk directly to the engine room—likely a feature the *Planter* had. The pilot also could send signals using the boat's steam whistles, which on the *Planter* were attached to two exhaust pipes behind the pilothouse.

The *Planter* was in many ways a fairly standard steamboat. But with Robert Smalls in the pilothouse, it was destined for a place in history.

CHAPTER FIVE
THE ESCAPE

Day after day Robert watched and listened. In the spring of 1862, an opportunity arose. The *Planter*'s crew was to move four cannons guarding a river southwest of Charleston to a fort being built in the harbor. The captain wanted the move completed by dark on Monday, May 12. The officers planned to go ashore that night and stay until morning.

Robert realized this was the chance he had been waiting for.

On May 12, the *Planter* traveled to the river to transfer the cannons. Robert and his crewmates knew how valuable these weapons would be to the Union. They planned to delay the delivery of the cannons and escape with them.

The men purposely worked slowly. They fumbled knots and dropped lines. By the time all four cannons were on board it was late afternoon. Robert's plan was working. Delivery to the fort would have to wait until morning.

Robert's mind raced as he guided the *Planter* back to its dock in the harbor.

The time for the escape was nearing. Throbbing with **anticipation**, he was careful not to let his excitement show.

Finally the officers went ashore, trusting Robert to have the boat ready for an early start in the morning.

Robert immediately gathered the crew and went over the plan once more. Then the men sprang into action, loading stacks of fire-wood on deck to power the steam boilers and double-checking every instrument. Robert put on a white ruffled shirt, a checked dress jacket, and the captain's wide-brimmed straw hat.

It was three o'clock in the morning by the time a full head of steam hissed in the boilers. The Confederate and South Carolina flags were raised to the top of the mast. In the pilothouse Robert gripped the wheel as he backed the *Planter* away from its dock in front of Confederate head-quarters. The ship coasted upstream a short way and stopped. A rowboat stole from the *Planter* to

fetch the families of the crew from a boat they had hidden in since nightfall.

Robert peered uneasily at the dark water, waiting for the rowboat to return with its precious load. After a few long minutes, it appeared. In pin-drop quiet the families boarded and were led below deck.

With everyone safely aboard, Robert started down the harbor. He blew the whistle to leave the dockside, and it was answered. Fighting a strong urge to rush, Robert eased the boat cautiously into the open water. He had to remain calm. His family and the others on board were all counting on him.

Robert's patience paid off. The shore guard saw the *Planter* leave but did not stop it.

The *Planter*'s paddle wheels cut through the dark water with a steady churn. Castle Pinckney and Fort Ripley were passed easily. Fort Johnson loomed ahead, its walls bristling with cannons. His palms sweaty, Robert reached for the cord of the steam whistle. He blew the secret signal and prayed. The lookout signaled back: *All right.* Robert breathed a sigh of relief.

As the boat neared the massive walls of Fort Sumter, Robert saw that dawn was breaking. The *Planter* had lost time bucking the incoming tide. In the early-morning light, the lookout might be able to tell that Robert was not the captain. An anxious crewmate told Robert to make a dash for freedom. But Robert knew that if the *Planter* sped by the fort, cannons would be fired on them, smashing the boat to pieces. He continued at the slow, even speed the guards expected.

Robert asked a crewmate to take the wheel. He

pulled down the captain's straw hat to shadow his face and stood at the window of the pilothouse. Under his fancy jacket Robert's heart thumped loudly. Mimicking the captain, he folded his arms across his chest. Then slowly Robert sounded the signal—*WOOOOO, WOOOOO, WOO!*

From the pilothouse to the engine room to the hold, bodies tensed. The response was taking too long. . . . Then, finally, the *Planter* received the signal to pass. Robert mopped sweat from his brow. There were only a few more miles to go and one more fort to pass.

CHAPTER SIX
FULL STEAM AHEAD

Fort Moultrie came up quickly, and the *Planter* passed without trouble. Robert kept the same **deliberate** pace until the boat was out of range of the last Confederate gun. Then he ordered FULL STEAM AHEAD! Clouds of black smoke belched from the smokestack. The boat surged forward, its paddle wheels whisking the water white.

A Confederate lookout saw the burst of speed through his field glasses. When the boat headed out to sea, he knew something was wrong. Frantically

the
lookout
signaled
an alert. Lights
flashed and flick-
ered, but it was too late.
No Confederate guns could
reach the *Planter* now.

The Union ships and freedom waited just ahead, but the *Planter* still was not safe. From the beginning Robert had worried most about these final moments. Union sailors would be ready to fire on any boat coming from Charleston. Robert had to convince them not to shoot. Ordering the flags lowered and Hannah's best white sheet raised as a sign of surrender, Robert sailed toward the *Onward*, the nearest ship of the Union fleet. In the early morning fog, the Union lookout couldn't see the white sheet. He saw only a big boat speeding through the haze and mist. He thought it was a Confederate vessel coming to ram them.

The lookout shouted an alarm, and the *Onward* turned, pointing a row of guns at the *Planter*. Leaning hard on the wheel, Robert swung the boat around. With the turn the white sheet caught the wind and flapped open in the ocean breeze. Suddenly a Union sailor cried out that he saw a white flag.

The *Onward*'s captain ordered the gunners to hold their fire and instructed the *Planter* to come alongside.

Men, women, and children ran out onto the deck of the *Planter*. Robert, standing straight and proud, stepped forward and raised the captain's hat high in the air. He shouted that he had brought the Union a load of Confederate cannons.

When the *Onward*'s surprised captain climbed aboard, Robert told him he thought the *Planter* might be of some service to "Uncle Abe" Lincoln. Then Robert turned the Confederate boat and its cannons over to the Union navy.

The white sheet was lowered. As the *Planter*'s crew and their families gazed up, the Union flag rose skyward. Robert and Hannah held their children close, their hearts full of hope. On this morning of a new day, they were on their way to freedom.

The Wedding Chest Escape

Eighteen-year-old Lear Green struggled with her emotions when William Adams asked her to marry him in 1857. She wanted to say "yes," but a huge fear stopped her.

William was free and a barber by trade, but Lear was enslaved. She belonged to the family of James Noble, a butter merchant in Baltimore, Maryland. Noble had inherited her from his wife's mother when Lear was a very young girl. Lear barely remembered her first mistress, but she found Noble and his wife "very exacting and oppressive . . . with no **disposition** whatever to allow her any liberties."

By the time Lear became a teenager, she knew that any children she had would belong to her master. She also knew that enslaved children, as property, could be sold away from their parents. She couldn't bear to let that happen. Lear discussed her fears with William and their mothers. All agreed that she had to be free before they could marry. Finally, they came up with

This 1872 illustration shows Lear Green escaping in her chest.

a daring and very risky plan. They decided William's mother, who was free and lived in Elmira, New York, would come to Baltimore for a visit. Meanwhile, they found an old, large, sturdy sailor's chest.

On a steamy Sunday in May 1857, a quilt, pillow, and a few clothes were placed in the chest, along with a little food and water. Lear squeezed in, and the box was tied shut with strong ropes. Two men carried the chest to the docks of the Philadelphia-bound Ericsson Line steamboat. The box was loaded on deck with the ordinary **freight**.

The boat's rules dictated that William's mother, as a black person, had to travel on the deck rather than inside. And that is exactly where she wanted to be! She kept a close eye on the chest. Twice during the dark night, she edged close and lifted the lid slightly to give Lear fresh air. Lear had to remain perfectly quiet inside the hot chest. If she sneezed or coughed, she might be found out.

The journey dragged on and on—for eighteen hours. Finally, the steamer landed in Philadelphia. This marked an especially dangerous moment in the plan. Someone might drop the chest and injure Lear, or get suspicious about the chest's weight.

Luckily, all went smoothly and the chest arrived at the home of family friends. From there, Lear was taken to the home of William Still, an avid **abolitionist** in Philadelphia. He would later write down her story in his book *The Underground Railroad*. Despite the peril Lear faced, she told him "she had no fear."

After some time with the Still family, Lear traveled to Elmira, New York, a stop on the Underground

Railroad between Philadelphia and Ontario, Canada. Lear and William had planned to go on to Canada, but they stayed in Elmira, where there was a community of free blacks. The young couple wed and had a daughter, Elizabeth. In freedom, Lear took the name Elizabeth J. Adams, likely to prevent her capture.

James Noble ran an ad in *The Sun*, a Baltimore newspaper, offering a reward of $150 for Lear's return. But the young woman remained safe. Sadly, just three years after her escape, Elizabeth Adams died of tuberculosis. She is buried in Woodlawn Cemetery in Elmira. She was honored in 2009 by the Elmira **Juneteenth** Committee with a program telling her story and in 2010 with the dedication of a marker for her grave.

CHAPTER SEVEN
A NATIONAL HERO

While the South fumed over the loss of the *Planter*, the North praised Robert Smalls as a national hero. The *New York Herald* declared his action "one of the most heroic and daring adventures since the war **commenced**." Robert was employed as a civilian pilot for the Union navy. He met with President Lincoln and helped convince him to let African Americans enlist in the Union army. Robert spoke to crowds in the North to gain aid for those formerly enslaved.

On December 1, 1863, Robert had another adventure aboard the *Planter*. He was piloting the boat for the Union when it came under intense fire in South Carolina. The captain ordered Robert to

surrender the boat, then hid in the coal **bunker**. Knowing the crew of former enslaved people could be killed if captured, Robert took the wheel and steered to outrun the Confederates. For his heroism Robert was named the *Planter*'s captain, making him the first African American captain of a United States vessel.

Throughout the war Robert piloted several Union ships, taking part in seventeen battles. He was consistently supported by his fellow black people, military leaders, abolitionists, and others both in the North and South. Yet he still had to fight against discrimination. When he was in Philadelphia in 1864, securing repairs for the *Planter*, he was told to surrender his seat on a streetcar to a white passenger. He left the streetcar rather than stand on the open platform in the rain.

During the war years, Hannah gave birth to the couple's second daughter, Sarah. Sadly, their son, Robert Jr., died of smallpox. The family also included Robert's stepdaughters, Charlotte and Clara Jones, born to Hannah before the couple met. Clara, a teenager at the time of the *Planter* escape, braved the risky journey with the family. Charlotte stayed behind with her five-year-old daughter, Emily, and Emily's father.

Robert and his family remained in Beaufort after the war. He purchased the McKee house, hired a tutor to improve his reading and writing skills, and was a founder of the Republican Party in South Carolina. In 1868, along with seventy-six African Americans and forty-eight whites, Robert helped write a new democratic state constitution. His proposal on education became part of the new document. It called for the creation of South Carolina's first free system of public schools for all children. Robert was so popular in the heavily black area where he lived that his enemies referred to him as the "king of Beaufort County." With this popularity, he won seats in both the state house and senate, where he fought for equal rights for African Americans. He was active in the state **militia** and rose to the rank of major general.

Robert became a United States congressman in 1875 and served for five terms. He called for the **elimination** of race discrimination in the army, introduced a petition to give women the right to vote, and fought against separate railroad cars for African Americans. He was one of sixteen black men to serve in Congress during **Reconstruction**, and while they worked together closely, he still faced a great deal of racism and bigotry from whites. He was forced to leave at least two hotels because of the color of his skin, one in South Carolina and another in Boston. A group of racist whites in South Carolina, called the Red Shirts, often threatened Robert's life.

After his congressional career ended in 1887, Robert was appointed collector of customs in Beaufort, a position he held, with one break, for almost twenty years. Hannah died in 1883.

Robert later married a woman named Annie Wigg and had another son, William (Willie).

In 1895 South Carolina revised its state constitution and legally restricted the right of African Americans to vote—a right that had been granted by an amendment to the United States Constitution in 1870. Robert, one of only six African American delegates to the 1895 constitutional convention, argued eloquently to preserve his people's right to vote. Still, the right was all but taken away by the many limitations placed on it. Robert and other African American delegates refused to sign the document to adopt these changes. With the rights of African Americans slipping away, Robert continued to fight unfair southern laws by giving speeches and reaching out to members of the US Congress.

In his later years Robert often visited with African American students in Beaufort. He told them about the accomplishments of their people and stressed the importance of education. Robert died in 1915 at the age of seventy-five. His funeral was the largest ever held in Beaufort.

In 2004 the United States Army christened the *Major General Robert Smalls*. This ship is the first army vessel ever named after an African American. Six years later, researchers found what they believe to be the remains of the *Planter* off Cape Romain Island in South Carolina. The *Planter* was wrecked in 1876 as it tried to rescue another boat that had gone aground. Possible further testing is on hold pending funding. A statue of US Congressman Robert Smalls now stands in the National Museum of African American History and Culture, which opened in Washington, DC, in September 2016.

On another statue, near Robert Smalls's grave in Beaufort, are his words from the 1895 constitutional convention:

"My race needs no special defense, for the past history of them in this country proves them to be the equal of any people. All they need is an equal chance in the battle of life."

TIMELINE

1839 April 5: Born in Beaufort, South Carolina, to Lydia Polite, an enslaved woman, and an unknown man

1851 The McKees send him to live in Charleston, South Carolina, where he works at the Planter's Hotel

1854 Becomes foreman of a crew on the Charleston docks

1856 December 24: Marries Hannah Jones, a Charleston hotel maid

1858 February 12: Daughter Elizabeth Lydia Smalls born

1861 Son Robert Smalls Jr. born

April 12–13: The battle of Fort Sumter launches the Civil War

1862 May 13: Robert and his fellow enslaved crew steal the *Planter*, pick up their families, navigate the boat out of Confederate waters, and turn it over to the US Navy

Works as a civilian with the US Navy, piloting boats and removing Confederate mines in the water

1863 Robert Smalls Jr. dies of smallpox

November: Transferred to the US Army

December 1: Daughter Sarah Vorhees Smalls born

December 1: Becomes the first African American captain of a United States vessel after piloting the *Planter* through enemy waters and narrowly evading Confederate capture

1864 January: Purchases the McKee house in Beaufort, South Carolina

May: Voted a delegate to the Republican National Convention, but cannot attend because of military duties

Learns to read during a stay in Philadelphia

June or July: Forced to give up streetcar seat to a white person in Philadelphia

1865 April 9: The South surrenders, ending the Civil War. Robert later pilots the *Planter*, overloaded with blacks and whites, to the ceremonial raising of the American flag at Fort Sumter

1866 September: Service with US Army ends

1867 Opens a store and school for freed enslaved people

1868 Elected to the South Carolina House of Representatives

Participates in writing a new state constitution for South Carolina

1870 Elected to the South Carolina Senate

1872 Begins to publish a newspaper, the *Beaufort Southern Standard*

1874 Elected to the US House of Representatives, where he serves first until 1879 and again from 1882–1887, becoming the second-longest-serving African American in Congress for many decades

1883 July 28: Wife Hannah Jones Smalls dies

1889 Appointed collector of the port of Beaufort, a post he holds until 1892

Marries Annie Wigg, a Charleston schoolteacher

1892 Son William Robert Smalls born

1895 Argues against a revised South Carolina state constitution that limited African American voting rights, ultimately refusing to sign it

November 5: Wife Annie Smalls dies

1897 Granted a pension of $30 a month—the pension for a Navy captain—by a special act of Congress

1898 Reappointed collector of the port of Beaufort, serving until 1913

1915 February 23: Dies of complications of diabetes

GLOSSARY

abolish (uh-BOL-ish) *verb* to end something

abolitionist (ab-uh-LISH-uh-nist) *noun* a person who is against slavery

agricultural (AG-ri-kul-chur-ul) *adjective* relating to growing crops or raising animals

anticipation (an-TISS-uh-pay-shun) *noun* the act of thinking about or looking forward to an event in the future

auction (AWK-shun) *adjective* referring to a public sale where buyers bid money for items

blockade (blah-KADE) *noun* a group of ships positioned to block other ships from approaching a port or coast

bunker (BUN-kur) *noun* a bin or large container for storing fuel

cargo (kar-GO) *noun* goods carried by a truck, boat, or plane

channels (CHAN-uhls) *noun* strips of water between land areas

chattel slavery (CHAT-uhl SLAY-vur-ee) *noun* a form of slavery in which enslaved people are considered property that can be inherited or sold

commence (kuh-MENS) *verb* to start

commercially (kuh-MUR-shuhl-ee) *adverb* in a way related to business

Confederate States of America (kun-FED-ur-it STATES UV uh-MER-i-kuh) *noun* group of southern states that left the United States to form their own government in support of slavery, starting the Civil War

constitution (kon-sti-TOO-shun) *noun* rules that guide how a country works

deliberate (di-LIB-ur-it) *adjective* slow and steady

disposition (dis-puh-ZISH-un) *noun* usual way of acting; mood

divisive (di-VIE-siv) *adjective* tending to cause disagreement

economy (ee-KON-uh-mee) *noun* the way a country produces, distributes, and uses its resources

elimination (ee-lim-uh-NAY-shun) *noun* the act of getting rid of something

field hands (FEELED HANDS) *noun* persons who plant, weed, and harvest crops

foreman (FOR-mun) *noun* the head of a group of workers

freight (FRATE) *noun* goods carried on a truck, boat, or plane

fugitive (FEW-ji-tiv) *adjective* having run away or escaped

garment (GAR-ment) *noun* item of clothing

inauguration (in-AW-guh-RAY-shun) *noun* ceremony to put a person in office

indentured servant (in-DEN-tured SUR-vunt) *noun* person bound by an agreement to work for another for a set period of time to pay off a debt

industrialized (in-DUS-tree-uh-lized) *adjective* making products on a large scale using people and machines

Juneteenth (JOON-TEENTH) *adjective* relating to the day celebrating the emancipation of the enslaved in Texas on June 19, 1865

justify (JUS-tuh-fie) *verb* to explain or prove that something is right or fair

lease (LEES) *verb* to rent something under a written agreement

militia (mi-LISH-uh) *noun* group of citizens trained to fight in emergencies

navigate (NAV-i-gate) *verb* to steer

penalize (PEE-nuh-lize) *verb* to punish

planter (PLAN-tur) *noun* an owner of a large farm worked by laborers who live on the property

prestige (pre-STEEJ) *noun* high regard by others

Reconstruction (ree-kon-STRUK-shun) *proper noun* the period from 1863 to 1877, during which the United States tried to secure full civil rights for the formerly enslaved while reintegrating the Confederate states into the Union

reef (REEF) *noun* a ridge of sand or rock

rig (RIG) *verb* arranging the ropes and chains of a ship to support its masts and adjust its sails

secede (si-SEED) *verb* to leave

territories (TER-uh-tor-eez) *noun* areas of land under the control of the United States but not yet states

truce (TROOS) *noun* a temporary stop in fighting

wharf (WARF) *noun* long structure built near a body of water where ships can dock and load or unload cargo

TEXT SOURCES

A.M.E. Review, "Capt. Robert Smalls Addresses the General Conference of 1864," no. 70 (January–March, 1955): 22–23, 31.

Blassingame, John W., ed. "Robert Smalls," *Slave Testimony: Two Centuries of Letters, Speeches, Interviews, and Autobiographies.* Baton Rouge, LA: Louisiana State University Press, 1977.

Charleston Daily Courier, "The Steamer Planter," May 14, 1862.

Cowley, Charles. *The Romance of History in The Black County, and the Romance of War in the Career of Gen. Robert Smalls, The Hero of the* Planter. Lowell, MA: 1882.

Du Pont, Samuel Francis. *Samuel Francis Du Pont: A Selection from His Civil War Letters*, ed. John D. Hayes, Vol. 2. Ithaca, NY: Cornell University Press, 1969.

Guthrie, James M. "Camp-Fires of the Afro-American, 1889." In *The Negro's Civil War : How American Negroes Felt and Acted During the War for the Union* by James M. McPherson. New York: Ballantine Books, 1991.

Letters of William Robert Smalls to Dorothy Sterling 1955–1956, Amistad Research Center, Tulane University, New Orleans.

Miller, Edward A., Jr., *Gullah Statesman*. Columbia, SC: University of South Carolina Press, 1995.

New York Daily Tribune, "Robert Smalls, the Negro Pilot," September 10, 1862.

New York Herald, "Heroism of Nine Colored Men," May 18, 1862.

Sterling, Dorothy. *Captain of the* Planter. New York: Pocket Books, 1968.

US House of Representatives. Committee on Naval Affairs. *Authorizing the President to Place Robert Smalls on the Retired List of the Navy*, 47th Cong., 2d sess., Jan. 23, 1883. Reprinted 1887 in *Men of Mark* by William J. Simmons. Cleveland, OH: Geo. M. Rewell & Co., 1887.

US Naval War Records Office. *Official Records of the Union and Confederate Navies in the War of the Rebellion*. Washington, DC: Govt. Printing Office, 1894–1922, series I, vol. 12: 820–826. Series 2, vol. I: 180.

US War Dept., *The War of the Rebellion: a Compilation of the Official Records of the Union and Confederate Armies*, Washington, DC: Govt. Printing Office, 1880–1901, series I, vol. 14: 13–15, 502–503, 506, 509.

Uya, Okon Edet. *From Slavery to Public Service: Robert Smalls 1839–1915*. New York: Oxford University Press, 1971.

Washington, J. Irwin, Sr. "General Robert Smalls," *Colored American Magazine*, vol. 7 (June 1904): 424–31.

SIDEBAR SOURCES

SLAVERY

Boston, Nicholas. "The Slave Experience: Living Conditions." Slavery and the Making of America. https://www.thirteen.org/wnet/slavery/experience/living/history.html.

Bourne, Jenny. "Slavery in the United States." EH.net (Economic History Association). https://eh.net/encyclopedia/slavery-in-the-united-states/.

Collier, Christopher, and James Lincoln Collier. *Slavery and the Coming of the Civil War: 1831–1861*. New York: Benchmark Books: Marshall Cavendish, 2000.

"Conditions of Antebellum Slavery 1830–1860." PBS. https://www.pbs.org/wgbh/aia/part4/4p2956.html.

Gates, Henry Louis, Jr. "Did African-American Slaves Rebel?" The African Americans: Many Rivers to Cross. PBS. https://www.pbs.org/wnet/african-americans-many-rivers-to-cross/history/did-african-american-slaves-rebel/.

"Indentured Servants in Colonial Virginia," Encyclopedia Virginia. https://www.encyclopediavirginia.org/ Indentured_Servants_in_Colonial_Virginia.

Kamma, Anne. *If You Lived When There Was Slavery in America*. New York: Scholastic, 2004.

McPherson, James M. *Fields of Fury*. New York: Atheneum Books for Young Readers, 2002.

"Myths and Misunderstandings: Slavery in the United States." The American Civil War Museum. https://acwm.org/blog/myths-and-misunder standings-slavery-united-states.

"The Peculiar Institution: Slave Life and Slave Codes." U.S. History. http://www.ushistory.org/us/27b.asp.

Ransom, Roger L. "The Economics of the Civil War." EH.net (Economic History Association). https://eh.net/encyclopedia/ the-economics-of-the-civil-war/.

"Slavery in the American South." Constitutional Rights Foundation. http://www.crf-usa.org/ black-history-month/ slavery-in-the-american-south.

"U.S. Constitution: Constitutional Topic: Slavery." https://www.usconstitution.net/consttop_slav.html.

SAILING SHIPS IN THE 1800S

Coker, P.C. III. *Charleston's Maritime Heritage, 1670–1865.* Charleston, SC: CokerCraft Press, 1987.

"Elements of a Ship." Museum of American Heritage. http://www.moah.org/modelships/elements.html.

"History of Ships." Encyclopedia Britannica. https://www.britannica.com/technology/ship/History-of-ships.

Tibbetts, John H., "Rise and Fall and Rise . . . South Carolina's Maritime History." *Coastal Heritage*, Fall 2002. https://www.scseagrant.org/wp-content/uploads/Coastal-Heritage-Fall-2002.pdf.

"The Crew." Penobscot Marine Museum. https://penobscotmarinemuseum.org/pbho-1/life-at-sea/crew.

Wilkinson, Philip. *The World of Ships.* Boston: Kingfisher, 2005.

WHAT CAUSED THE CIVIL WAR?

Collier, Christopher, and James Lincoln Collier. *Slavery and the Coming of the Civil War: 1831–1861.* New York: Benchmark Books/Marshall Cavendish, 2000.

Collier, Christopher, and James Lincoln Collier. *The Civil War: 1860–1865*. New York: Benchmark Books/ Marshall Cavendish, 2000.

McPherson, James M. *Fields of Fury*. New York: Atheneum Books for Young Readers, 2002.

Naden, Corinne J., and Rose J. Blue. *Why Fight? The Causes of the American Civil War*. Austin, TX: Raintree Steck-Vaughn, 2004.

"Trigger Events of the Civil War." American Battlefield Trust. https://www.battlefields.org/learn/articles/trigger-events-civil-war.

THE *PLANTER*

"A History of Steamboats." https://www.sam.usace.army.mil/Portals/46/docs/recreation/OP-CO/montgomery/pdfs/10thand11th/ahistoryofsteamboats.pdf.

Billingsley, Andrew. *Yearning to Breathe Free*. Columbia, SC: University of South Carolina Press, 2007.

Cannady, Dennis. Phone call with author. April 20, 2019 and May 15, 2019.

Lineberry, Cate. *Be Free or Die*. New York: St. Martin's Press, 2017.

Steamboats.org. http://www.steamboats.org/index.php.

Terrell, Bruce G. E-mail correspondence with author. April 25, 2019.

Terrell, Bruce G., Gordon P. Watts, and Timothy J. Runyan. *The Search for Planter: The Ship that Escaped Charleston and Carried Robert Smalls to Destiny.* National Marine Sanctuaries, National Oceanic and Atmosphere Administration, May 2014.

THE WEDDING CHEST ESCAPE

DeRamus, Betty. "The Special Delivery Package." *Forbidden Fruit: Love Stories from the Underground Railroad.* New York: Atria Books, 2005.

Knowlton, Carole. E-mail correspondence with author. April 20, 2019.

Still, William. "Escaping in a Chest," *The Underground Railroad.* Chicago: Johnson Publishing Company, 1970.

Wagner, Tricia Martineau. *It Happened on the Underground Railroad.* Guilford, CT: Morris Book Publishing, 2007.

RECOMMENDED FURTHER READING

Fiction books are marked with an asterisk (*).

SLAVERY

* Anderson, Laurie Halse. *Chains*. Seeds of America Trilogy. New York: Atheneum Books for Young Readers, 2008.

* Bryan, Ashley. *Freedom Over Me: Eleven Slaves, Their Lives and Dreams Brought to Life*. New York: Atheneum Books for Young Readers/Caitlyn Dlouhy Books, 2016.

* Draper, Sharon. *Copper Sun*. New York: Atheneum Books for Young Readers, 2006.

Halfmann, Janet. *Midnight Teacher*. Illustrated by London Ladd. New York: Lee & Low Books, 2018.

* Lester, Julius. *Day of Tears*. Reprint edition. New York: Hyperion Books for Young Readers, 2007.

Lester, Julius. *To Be a Slave*. Illustrated by Tom Feelings. Reprint edition. New York: Puffin Modern Classics, 2005.

Weatherford, Carole Boston. *Freedom in Congo Square*. Illustrated by R. Gregory Christie. New York: little bee books, 2016.

ESCAPES FROM SLAVERY

* Curtis, Christopher Paul. *Elijah of Buxton*. New York: Scholastic Press, 2007.

Dunbar, Erica Armstrong, and Kathleen Van Cleeve. *Never Caught, The Story of Ona Judge: George and Martha Washington's Courageous Slave Who Dared to Run Away*. New York: Aladdin/Simon & Schuster, 2019.

* Evans, Shane W. *Underground: Finding the Light to Freedom*. New York: Roaring Brook Press, 2011.

Levine, Ellen. *Henry's Freedom Box: A True Story from the Underground Railroad*. Illustrated by Kadir Nelson. New York: Scholastic Press, 2007.

SAILING SHIPS

* Avi. *The True Adventures of Charlotte Doyle*. Reprint edition. New York: Scholastic Inc., 2012.

McKissack, Patricia C., and Frederick McKissack. *Black Hands, White Sails*. New York: Scholastic Press, 1999.

* Moss, Tamara. *Lintang and the Pirate Queen*. New York: Clarion Books, 2019.

* Preus, Margie. *Heart of a Samurai*. New York: Amulet Books, 2010.

ABOUT THE AUTHOR

JANET HALFMANN is the author of more than forty books for children, including Lee & Low's *Midnight Teacher*, which *Kirkus* called "An excellent homage to an African-American woman who taught ahead of her time" in a starred review. When she's not writing, Halfmann enjoys working in the garden, exploring nature, visiting new places, especially wildlife areas and living-history museums, and watching movies. Halfmann lives with her husband in South Milwaukee, Wisconsin. Find out more about her and her books at janethalfmannauthor.com.

ABOUT THE ILLUSTRATOR

DUANE SMITH is an artist, illustrator, and graphic designer with a degree from Pratt Institute in New York City and a Master's in Illustration from the Fashion Institute of Technology. His wide-ranging works have been featured in periodicals, books, movie storyboards, and galleries. Smith also works in graphic design and interactive media development, and splits his time between homes in Brooklyn and Albany, New York. Visit him online at http://www.dsmithillustration.com/.

PHOTO CREDITS